Art Therapy Exercises

by the same author

Art Therapy – The Person-Centred Way
Art and the Development of the Person
2nd edition
Liesl Silverstone
Foreword by Brian Thorne
ISBN 978 1 85302 481 8

of related interest

Art Therapy and Anger
Edited by Marian Liebmann
ISBN 978 1 84310 425 4

The Creative Arts in Palliative Care
Edited by Nigel Hartley and Malcolm Payne
ISBN: 978 1 84310 591 6

The Expressive Arts Activity Book
A Resource for Professionals
Suzanne Darley and Wende Heath
Illustrated by Mark Darley
Foreword by Gene D Cohen MD PhD
ISBN 978 1 84310 861 0

Little Windows into Art Therapy
Small Openings for Beginning Therapists
Deborah Schroder
ISBN 978 1 84310 778 1

Art Therapy and Clinical Neuroscience
Edited by Noah Hass-Cohen and Richard Carr
Foreword by Frances F Kaplan
ISBN 978 1 84310 868 9

A Creative Guide to Exploring Your Life
Self-Reflection Using Photography, Art, and Writing
Graham Gordon Ramsay and Holly Barlow Sweet
ISBN: 978 1 84310 892 4

Focusing-Oriented Art Therapy
Accessing the Body's Wisdom and Creative Intelligence
Laury Rappaport
ISBN 978 1 84310 760 6

Art Therapy Exercises

Inspirational and Practical Ideas to Stimulate the Imagination

Liesl Silverstone

Foreword by Brian Thorne

Jessica Kingsley Publishers
London and Philadelphia

First published in 2009
by Jessica Kingsley Publishers
116 Pentonville Road
London N1 9JB, UK
and
400 Market Street, Suite 400
Philadelphia, PA 19106, USA

www.jkp.com

Library of Congress Cataloging in Publication Data
Silverstone, Liesl.
  Art therapy exercises : inspirational and practical ideas to stimulate the imagination /
Liesl Silverston, Brian Thorne.
     p. ; cm.
  ISBN 978-1-84310-695-1 (pb : alk. paper) 1. Art therapy--Problems, exercises, etc. I.
Thorne, Brian, 1937- II. Title.
  [DNLM: 1. Art Therapy--methods. 2. Nondirective Therapy--methods. WM 450.5.A8
S587ab 2009]
  RC489.A7S547 2009
  616.89'1656--dc22

                           2008032774

British Library Cataloguing in Publication Data
A CIP catalogue record for this book is available from the British Library

ISBN 978 1 84310 695 1

Printed and bound in Great Britain by
Athenaeum Press, Gateshead, Tyne and Wear

*For the tutors of person-centred
art therapy skills courses past, present and future
With love*

'Imagination is more important than knowledge'

Albert Einstein

Contents

FOREWORD

    Brian Thorne 11

Introduction 15

Warm-up Exercises 26

    Mime/change object 27

    Toothpaste..................................... 28

1. Art Therapy Exercises for One-to-One Sessions and to Explore Individually in Groups 29

Exercises with explanations 31

    Magic carpet................................... 31

    Parcel 32

    Cave 33

    Path: Wood–wall–door 34

    Lost Property office 35

    Magic paintbook................................ 36

    Lucky dip...................................... 37

    Train journey 38

    Theatre.. 39

    Hot air balloon 40

The magic gift shop 40

Wise old person 42

Circle walk 44

Box 45

Fancy dress party 46

More exercises 47

Photo album 48

Car boot sale 48

River bank 49

A walk 49

Computer 50

The lighthouse 50

Art exhibition 51

Pond 52

A walk on the beach 52

A bird 53

An animal 53

A castle 53

Winter walk 54

Spring clean 54

Childhood memory 54

A relationship 55

A seed 55

A house 55

A tunnel 56

Separation, loss, change 56

Toyshop 57

Image in the round 57

Walk-sound 58

Pioneer 58

Space for your own exercises, ideas and comments   59

2. Art Therapy Exercises to Explore Individual Issues and Group Dynamics 61

Exercises 62
    Circus 62
    A cake 63
    Swimming pool 64
    A house 65
    Once upon a time 66
    Mandala 67

Space for your own exercises, ideas and comments   69

3. Further Inspiration for Art Therapy Exercises 71

Exercises 73
    The tree 74
    A conversation without words 74

Calendar-based exercises 75
    An Easter egg hunt 77
    Jewish Passover 77

Exercises using different materials 78
    Plasticine 79
    An object 80
    Buttons 81
    Picture postcards 82
    Collage 82

Space for your own exercises, ideas and comments   83

4. Working with Different Clients 85

Art therapy with children 85

    Peter 86

    Derek 87

    Trudy 88

    Linda.. 89

Art therapy with adults with learning
difficulties... 90

5. Some Guided Fantasies Devised
by Students 95

A Final Word 111

Space for your own exercises, ideas and comments 112

Foreword

The sense I'm left with is of harvest time – the season of abundance, a time for garnering, the fruition of much patient caring, of sometimes unrelenting toil and, above all, of loving and committed hopefulness. Liesl Silverstone's new book – a kind of presenter's supplement to her highly acclaimed *Art Therapy the Person-Centred Way* – is the outcome of a personal and professional life dedicated to the celebration of the imagination and to an unshakeable belief in the resilience of the human spirit.

For Liesl, art therapy and the person-centred approach are much more than a powerful response to individual suffering and wounded lives. They are a means of ensuring that in an age beset by competitive materialism and cognitive arrogance, the capacity of human beings to dream dreams, to create new worlds and to enter into deep empathic communion with each other is nourished and fostered. The training experiences she created and facilitated, which continue as certificate and diploma courses in person-centred art therapy skills throughout the country, have become a continuing beacon of hope in a world where all too often what seems to count is the number of targets achieved or what can be measured in quantitative terms.

Liesl believes in the often hidden potential of the human person to move towards a fullness of living where imagination, intuition and the creative impulse share parity of esteem with cognitive ability and analytical thought. She trusts the inarticulate yearnings of those who cannot find words to convey their deepest desires and aspirations. She encourages those who have never painted or sketched or modelled to discover their creative ability and thereby to enter a world infinitely larger than the imprisoning context of their previous existence. Many of us perhaps pay lip-service to concepts of holistic integrity, but Liesl challenges therapists and clients alike to take the risk of moving beyond the boundaries of familiar terrain to discover the liberation and the excitement of exercising capacities which had previously remained dormant or unacknowledged. There was a period when I had the privilege of acting as consultant to her training courses. To visit her cohorts of students as they neared the end of their training was to be assured of a transformative experience and to have my own limited perceptions of reality extended and rendered more challenging and entrancing.

In the pages of this book readers will find a veritable cornucopia of exercises which have the potential to open up new vistas and to inspire imaginative journeys of great richness. They are an invitation to trust the process of letting go of limitations and to respond to the challenge of extending awareness even if this seems frightening or even a little crazy. Most of the exercises are devised by Liesl herself and have stood the test of application in her own training groups or therapeutic encounters. Simply to read them is itself a voyage of discovery, but for many trainers and therapists they will constitute a repertoire on which they can draw as from an inexhaustible well. I have no doubt, too, that they will serve as an inspirational stimulus for the creation of further exercises which will offer yet more possibilities for those who retain their faith in human beings to transcend the often unwelcome desert of our current culture. Liesl's life and work are an enduring symbol of the hope which lies beyond despair. For me she calls up the image of the rare flower in full bloom which appears through an unexpected crack in the concrete. I salute her and, with countless others, rejoice in having known her.

Brian Thorne
Emeritus Professor of Counselling at the University of East Anglia,
Professor of Education in the College of Teachers,
Co-founder of the Norwich Centre, Norwich

Introduction

Content

Many of my colleagues welcome the idea of a manual of art therapy exercises to enrich and replenish their repertoires – so here goes!

The bulk of this book lists some 80 exercises (all applied, all experienced and most devised by me), with guidelines in offering them, advice for devising your own exercises – the *when*, *where*, *how* and *how not to*. The book is not about the facilitating of the ensuing image – my previous book *Art Therapy the Person-Centred Way* is for that – but is about the presenting.

There are sections on exercises for individuals, exercises for groups and group dynamic, various materials to use, focusing on dates in an inter-faith diary for inspiration, some examples of work with children and educationally disadvantaged adults, some exercises devised by students, and, importantly, several blank pages for the reader's own comments and ideas.

Training

Much emotive material can surface with image work. At present the practice of regulating the professions involved with human development is growing. Therefore, if readers are drawn to this field of work, it would be advisable to undertake some relevant training. There are diploma courses for those wishing to qualify as art therapists. For those with professional qualifications in therapeutic, educational, medical and social work settings who want to acquire skills in the therapeutic use of art, there are certificate and diploma courses in 'Person-Centred Art Therapy Skills' – the title approved by the Health Professions Council.

Adjusting to our multi-faith society

As well as relevant training, it is even more important for practitioners to be aware of the changing nature of our society in Great Britain and the Western world. We need to learn of the diverse ethnic and religious backgrounds and practices of our clients; without doing so, serious errors can and do occur in diagnostics and treatment. I believe that such education and understanding is vital – indeed needs to be mandatory – on all relevant training and re-training courses.

It may be necessary for the facilitator to undertake additional learning in this, and other, areas to keep abreast of changing times and needs. Qualification is the start, not the end, of the professional journey.

Art therapy

To become more integrated, we need to engage both verbal and non-verbal intelligence, both rational and intuitive knowing. Art therapy is one of the creative modes to keep us away from cerebral, verbal, judgemental processes, and in the here-and-now world of imagination, intuition, inspiration. The paradox applies that in thinking less it is possible to know more.

This learning process can be a safe, visible, keepable, accurate way towards self-awareness. Words (talking about) can have a once-removed flavour; images offer more immediacy, and may enable the client to be less self-conscious, more spontaneous, at every level of development. By making visible our images, we can tap into material from the subconscious denied to the forefront of our awareness, and gain valuable insights.

A spontaneous image can contain suppressed material, can have elements of hopes and fears; diverse aspects of the self, expressed symbolically, come to us from the subconscious, to be known, to be integrated. Images have very much the mysterious quality of dreams – something we fetch up from within, put out there, hardly knowing, at first, what they are about. We need to bring a kind of reverence, an awe, to our work with images. They have an aura of the 'as-yet-unknown', acquiring our respect.

Art is visible, keepable (unlike words, which we may forget) and can continue to offer up its meaning when we are ready to know it. We project something significant of ourselves onto an image. And in spontaneous 'Aha' moments, we know.

Working with an image can be safer than talking about 'me' – I am talking about me via the image, a gentler process than 'eyeball to eyeball'. Words become less censored, more spontaneous: 'right side of the brain' words, more likely to contain or reveal pertinent truths. An image is safe, as I am likely to see what I'm ready to see, at my pace. It may be quick; even in five minutes the essence of meaning can be revealed.

Images are a means of communicating for those with limited or impaired verbal skills, and for the articulate whose words can distract, defend, deceive. The spontaneous image is 'spot on'. It can be trusted.

The person-centred approach, working at the pace of the client, respects that time of readiness or unreadiness. If the client does not see what the picture shows, at this moment, the counsellor does not push, intrude; rather, accepts, lets be, moves on. Perhaps later the client will be ready, will know. Perhaps not.

Person-centred approach

I favour bringing the person-centred approach to the therapeutic use of art: there are disciplines where the practitioner is directive, may interpret, may suggest the meaning to the client. In contrast, the person-centred way, based on the belief that the individual is responsible and capable of self-determination, enables the *client* to discover the message of the image, thus gaining self-awareness as well as moving towards a more autonomous way of being.

I remember, many, many years ago, when interpreting jarred for me: I was on a brief counselling course. I was required to tell my story in a one-to-one session with the facilitator. She gave me a lengthy interpretation. I was outraged and rejected it. Some four years on, in my therapy with a person-centred counsellor, I had reached a stage when I could own the interpretation of four years earlier, but at *my* pace, at *my* time of readiness.

Images are extensions of the self – made visible in symbolic art form. To have dialogue with such an image in a person-centred way, to reflect back aspects of the image – size, colour, position of shapes, use of material, the process of image-making, that which is missing – can help the client to connect, make bridges between the image and the self. Healing, growth and integration can occur at every level of development.

In my ideal world, every training course in the field of human development would have components of art therapy on their syllabus: from integrated courses to integrated practitioners to integrated clients!

Art therapy exercises

Western culture tends to focus largely on the left side of the brain: verbal, analytical, thinking, judging mode in its educational structures, ignoring the development of the right side of the brain: intuition, imagination, inspiration and creativity. By and large, we are born with imagination. As we go through school, this facility is sidelined, with emphasis on the intellect. Who will put 'I'm creative, spontaneous' on their CV, and if they do, to what avail?

When working with art therapy, we need to tap into our creative mode. To kick-start the process, to move the client from thinking to intuiting, we use art therapy exercises. I remember long ago being told that the gate between the left and right sides of my brain is rusty. Many years of image-work have oiled the gate, removed the rust and given me more balance between the two hemispheres.

So, an art therapy exercise needs to exclude thinking, criticizing, analysing, and be non-directive, to give the client the fullest scope to produce an image on his or her terms.

Offering an art therapy exercise

First of all, be sure you have the art material you need – or can have. Years ago, all I could have was a box of coloured pencils and a school notebook. Much amazing image work and insights ensued.

Similarly, it does not follow that more will emerge the more time you have. Very quick exercises can get to the crux fast, as we shall see later. Be sure the materials match the time and the number of participants you have. No good using paint if you work for one hour with a group of 12, each sharing their image. Think it through.

You need to be clear about your purpose: what are you offering, when and why? You have a responsibility to bring appropriate material. You do not begin an art exercise 15 minutes before the end of a session, with inadequate time to deal with the process. Timing is important: when to offer material; is the client – *are you* – sufficiently trusting to be open to a new initiative? If working in a group, allow equal time for sharing with the group members. Ensure there will be as little noise as possible, as few interruptions as possible. Be clear and level about your intentions. Don't 'hoodwink' someone into art therapy.

State to the group that there is to be no talking during the process – talking can shatter the image. Watch your pace – enough time to close the eyes, relax, quieten, before introducing the exercise. When offering an exercise, avoid the word 'think' ('Think of an animal' takes you to the left side of the brain). Rather, 'Let an image come up of…'.

Leave enough time for the imaging to occur. If offering a guided fantasy, allow sufficient time for each stage. Haste can be very disturbing. A common feature of the new facilitator is to rush.

I find it easier to enter the image world with eyes closed. Open eyes could look around, distract. To start, I might say something like:

'Close your eyes' (*pause*)

'Relax' (*pause*)

'Take some easy, regular breaths' (*pause*)

'Try to clear your mind of thoughts' (*pause*)

'Into this blank space, without thinking or censoring, allow an image to float up of...' (*lengthy pause*).

(*After some minutes*) 'Now, gently, open your eyes, convey your image in art-form, in whatever way is right for you' (*enough pause*).

For a guided fantasy, I might say:

'And now you find yourself in…' (*tell the fantasy slowly enough with apt pauses*).

Continue as before:

'Now, gently open your eyes…' and so on.

When making their picture, say how long the group has (five minutes, two minutes). Before the end, say 'You have one minute left to do whatever you need to finish.'

I will not repeat this format with each exercise given in the main section of the book.

Later, when working on a picture with a client, you sit side by side, with the picture before and between you – that way you can both participate equally in dialoguing with aspects of the picture.

To my mind there are four stages in image work:

1. Let the image come on your inner eye.

2. Make that image visible in art-form.

3. Explore that image with a facilitator.

4. Work through the ensuing meaning.

To illustrate: in an exercise offering the theme 'animal':

1. A tiger emerged.

2. A tiger was drawn.

3. The client said she was generally like a pussy cat and wished she could let her tiger aspect emerge when necessary.

4. Recognizing this message is not enough. The client needs to work on the pussy cat, and the need to contact her tiger, perhaps with an appropriate therapist, away from the session. If this work is not done, the message might return in other image work, until resolved.

The main purpose of this book is to dwell on points 1 and 2. Point 3, facilitating the image, to release its gift, its message is explored in my book *Art Therapy – the Person-Centred Way.*

Do not ignore Point 4, or else points 1–3 are not utilized, the scope and potential of the art work is not fulfilled.

Guided fantasies

Several disciplines use guided fantasy: the client follows a fantasy in his or her imagination, and then talks about it.

I find that by offering the additional component of conveying the fantasy to visible art form, much more material or insight can emerge. Before offering a guided fantasy for the first time, I would explain what it means and what can happen, and suggest that participants follow the fantasy and focus on aspects in whatever way is right for them.

Guided fantasies are used to stimulate the imagination. They can be applied fruitfully when working with art. The preamble tends to tell a story, leading you away from thinking, to a symbolic fantasy world, to the core of the story.

Two main errors can occur when offering such an exercise:

1. The facilitator is too directive, not giving the client fullest scope for his or her own image to emerge (like holding a mirror up to the client and putting the facilitator's image into the reflection).

2. The pace of talking can be too fast. This can be confusing and disturbing for the client: just as an image begins to surface, more guidelines are given. I tend to pace myself as I offer a guided fantasy by taking myself through it, only speaking the next bit when I've got hold of an image for the preceding bit. Better too slow than too fast!

A group exercise

These exercises are doubly helpful; first, to work with each person on an individual level and, second, to focus on each person and the group dynamics they carry for the group. On the group house exercise (see p.65) for example, the person who builds a fence around her house; the one who makes roads linking up with all the others; the one who adds a little island for herself – working with these aspects as the group dynamics can bring insights and bond the group.

Spontaneous imaging

Once the client's gate has been well-oiled with practice, and imaging becomes easy, images surface spontaneously, and art therapy exercises may not be needed.

'On the hoof' with art therapy

This tool has most scope for counsellors, psychotherapists and art therapists when working one-to-one: when you hear an emotive word, a feeling, person, symptom, then, quite spontaneously and without time to think, suggest an image of, say, betrayal, anger, the person or the symptom. This can lead to surprising shifts. Of course, you should have told the client earlier during the contract-making session that you might introduce image work, and gain their agreement to this.

Devising your own art therapy exercise

Just make sure the image is as open-ended and non-directive as possible. Leave out any 'thinking' elements; thoughts connect you with your awareness, the image would just show that which you know already.

Conclusion

Perusing the book, readers may reinforce their belief in the effectiveness of art therapy at every level of human development. Furthermore, readers have the opportunity to become ever more creative, insightful and intuitive, be they wearing the facilitator's hat, the client's hat, or both.

And now, the exercises!

WARM-UP EXERCISES

Numerous workshops in the area of self-awareness offer a warm-up exercise. These can help participants to relax, be more spontaneous and enjoy themselves. Here are two examples of warm-up exercises you might like to try.

Mime/change object

Participants stand in a circle. You, the facilitator, form an object in mime (e.g. a mouse) and pass it to a group member. You ask the group member to make it into something else and pass it to the next person. And so on, all the way round. Feed back.

Toothpaste

Participants stand in a circle. The facilitator says: 'Imagine you are holding a giant tube of toothpaste… What do you do?' Each shares.

In one group, one person wrote her name large on the mirror; another smeared toothpaste all over the wall, yet another squeezed it out of the window, and so on. Only one person put a little on a toothbrush and brushed his teeth!

Both exercises can stimulate the imagination.

CHAPTER 1

Art Therapy Exercises for One-to-One Sessions and to Explore Individually in Groups

The exercises that follow are intended to explore an individual's issues – whether in a one-to-one setting or within a group. A later section in the book will offer exercises to explore group dynamics.

Carl Rogers maintained that the most effective learning is that which is self-discovered (*Freedom to Learn*, 3rd edition, Prentice Hall, 1994, ISBN 9780024031211; *On Personal Power*, Constable and Robinson, 1978, ISBN 9780094620202). Based on much evidence and experience, this is a belief I share. Thus, the art therapy training courses I offer are in the main experiential, giving the student opportunities for self-discovered learning as a central part of their training. Many of the exercises in this book were offered to students studying person-centred art therapy skills.

Students would be offered an art therapy exercise, and portray the ensuing image. Then, each student would work with the image (either the tutor or a peer facilitating), thus leading to skills as practitioners and self-awareness as clients (proof of the pudding).

There are many other group setting in which image work may be explored individually: e.g. staff groups, families, women's groups, support groups for substance misuse and offenders. I trust that readers will apply the exercises appropriately to their settings and purpose.

In the introduction to this book, I made some suggestions on offering art therapy exercises. Here, I won't repeat the preamble, the ending nor the invitation to produce the image each time. I will describe the exercise itself, as if I'm offering it.

EXERCISES WITH EXPLANATIONS

Magic carpet

'You are sitting in this room...on a small carpet' (*pause*).

'Now, you notice that the carpet, with you on it, is rising slowly, floating towards the open window...(*pause*). You are floating out of the window...rising...up, up... You are flying over the rooftops...gently flying...(*longer pause*).

'Now, you notice that the carpet with you on it is slowly descending (*pause*) down, down. And now you have landed (*pause*). You look all around you (*pause*). What do you see? (*longer pause*) And now, gently, open your eyes. You are back in this room.

'Draw your experience, in whatever way is right for you (*pause*) You have about five minutes.'

(*After four minutes*) 'There is one minute left. Just be finishing off (*pause*). Now, stop.'

This exercise may be offered one-to-one or in a group, and may be worked on with each group member, one-to-one.

Whatever is around for you will be projected onto the image. The subconscious knows... You will know, when ready to know.

Parcel

'And now…you are at home (*pause*). You hear a knock on your front door (*pause*). You go to the door…you open it…you look about, you see no one…you look down…you see a package…it has your name on it.

'You pick it up and take it inside (*pause*).

'What are you doing? (*longer pause*).

'Now, open your eyes gently, and make visible your experience, whichever way is right for you, and so on.'

This exercise is good for one-to-one, and one-to-one in a group.

Because of our awareness of terrorism and unattended packages, I've had one student, who, when imaging this exercise, wouldn't touch the parcel, shut the door and called the police. (On a personal level, this also made the material relevant for her.) Everyone else, over the years, has brought the package in, opened it and discovered the content – usually the core of the exercise.

Cave

'And now, you find yourself on a path (*pause*) going gently up the side of a hill. You continue up this path (*pause*) and now…you reach the entrance of a cave (*pause*) you go in…you look about…you notice several doors in the cave wall…you go up to them…each has a name on it…you come to a door with your name on it…you open the door…you go in…you look around… What do you see? (*lengthy pause*).

'And now, gently open your eyes and come back to this room, and so on.'

This exercise, like most guided fantasies, takes a while to lead you from thinking to imaging mode, to a world of the imagination. The ensuing image is therefore more likely to contain relevant symbolic material.

Path: Wood-wall-door

'And now, you are on a path, in a wood (*pause*). You are looking around you, as you walk along this path...continue walking. Now, ahead of you, there is a wall...you go up to the wall. And you see a door in the wall. You open the door...and go through it... What do you see? (*longer pause*).

'Now, gently open your eyes, and so on.'

Again, the 'guided' part of the fantasy leads you to an entirely open-ended aspect where it's over to you. The 'guided' bit is a suggestion; you go with it, or go your own way. Whatever emerges, will be a relevant projection of *yours* in symbolic image form.

Lost Property office

'You are walking along a pavement past a parade of shops. You come to a shop front you do not recognize…there is a door…you are drawn to the door, and enter. There is a counter and a person behind it… They say: "Can I help you?" You ask: "Where am I?" They say: "This is a lost property office. Here is a form, do fill it in." You fill it in. The official goes away…and returns, carrying something. "This is yours," they say, and give it to you.

'What is it?' (*longer pause*).

Here, the object might well represent something of yours you've left behind, lost, couldn't or didn't keep, etc.

Magic paintbook

'You are looking at some books on a bookshelf. One stands out...you take it out. It says: "Magic paintbook" (*pause*). You fetch a jar of water and a paint-brush (*pause*). You sit down, open the book and brush water onto the page...

'What emerges?' (*pause long enough*).

Again, open-ended; what comes up is entirely yours.

Lucky dip

'You are walking around a bazaar looking at the stalls… You see a sign: "Lucky Dip" (*pause*). You go up to it. There is a tub full of sawdust… coloured ribbons emerge at the top… You decide to have a go…you pay…you select a ribbon…you pull (*longer pause*). A package is tied to the end of the ribbon…you open it… What do you find?' (*longer pause*).

Once more the guided fantasy leads you to an open-ended aspect, for you to fill in.

Train journey

'You are at the station. Your train is in (*pause*).
You get on, take a seat. The train leaves…it
travels, for a long time. Suddenly, the train stops
(*pause*). An announcement asks you to get out…
You do…you look about (*pause*). Where are
you?' (*longer pause*).

It can happen that a participant will focus on aspects of
the fantasy on the way, and develop these rather than continuing with the guided fantasy. Fine. Whatever emerges
can produce fruitful awareness when working with the
image.

Theatre

'You enter the lobby of a theatre (*pause*). You look at your ticket (*pause*). You go up the stairs to the dress circle (*pause*). You enter the dress circle.

'You go down the aisle to the row of your seat... you find your seat...you look about you (*pause*). The lights go down – the curtain goes up. What do you see?' (*longer pause*).

Hot air balloon

'And now, you are in a meadow, looking around you (*pause*). You look up…high up, you see a hot air balloon (*pause*). It is slowly descending… it lands on the meadow (*pause*). A figure emerges…and walks towards you… (*longer pause*)'

Here it could be that an issue around a relationship might emerge.

The magic gift shop

'Close your eyes (*pause*). You are walking along a street in a town (*pause*). You come to a side-street (*pause*). You have never been in this street before…you walk down the side-street (*pause*). You notice a shop…you look into the shop window. There are all kinds of objects from different times, different parts of the world…you go into the shop…

'The shopkeeper greets you, saying: "Do look around" (*pause*). Perhaps, as you look, you may be drawn to one object in particular…maybe you have noticed one such object. Take a good look at it (*pause*). Now the shopkeeper says: "This is an unusual shop. We don't take money. If you want the object for yourself, you need to exchange it for something of yours" (*pause*). And you are thinking what you might give up of yours, leave here, so that you can have the object of your choice.

'Now it is time for you to leave (*pause*). You go out of the shop. You're in the little side-street walking back to the main street (*pause*). Now, you're back in the street where you began (*pause*). When you are ready, open your eyes, come back to this room, and portray aspects of your journey, your visit to the shop, in whatever way seems right for you (*pause*). You have ten minutes (*longer pause*). You have one minute left...'

This exercise has the potential to reveal what you might need to relinquish in order to gain what you want. As in most art therapy, the message received will require more work from you – perhaps with a counsellor – to effect the desired change. *From knowing, to owning, to change.*

Wise old person

'And now, you are in a meadow, looking about you (*pause*). Looking across the meadow, you see a wood (*pause*). You have reached the edge of the wood, and you see a path going into the wood (*pause*). Now you are walking along the path, looking about you...ahead of you along the path, you see a clearing (*pause*). You have reached the clearing and you see a cottage...you are outside the cottage. You open the door and go in (*pause*). Looking about you, you see a wise old person, seemingly expecting you (*pause*). The wise old person says: "Is there something you want to ask me?" You are reflecting on what to ask (*pause*). You ask your question...and listen out for an answer (*pause*). How do you feel? Now, the wise old person says: "Before you go, I want to give you this gift" (*pause*). You receive the gift and look at it... How do you feel?

'It is time to say goodbye, one to the other. You leave the wise old person and the cottage (*pause*). You are back on the path through the wood...looking about you (*pause*). What do you see now? Now, you are back in the meadow, reflecting on your journey (*pause*). Now, open your eyes...and express in art-form your experience in whatever way is right for you.'

This is a guided fantasy of significant potential. Whenever you have an issue needing resolution, you could find your way to the wise old person *within yourself,* ask your question and receive an answer – a gift, often a relevant component. From darkness to enlightenment.

In opening this exercise, it is important to say 'wise old person', not 'wise old woman' or 'wise old man'. The gender is for the client to know, and can be significant.

Circle walk

The students form a circle and turn to the right. They are asked to walk round in a circle, taking regular, slow, rhythmic steps, looking at their feet, thinking of nothing, a meditative, quiet walk. As they walk on and on, see if an image emerges. When ready, stay with the image and portray it.

There is an opportunity to experience spontaneous imaging, without a specific 'prop' as a structure.

This activity may be best used with people who have done some image work already.

Box

'And now, you find yourself in a box…what
do you notice? (*good pause*). How do you feel?
(*pause*). What are you doing?

'It is now time for you to leave the box (*pause*).
You are outside the box…what do you do?
(*longer pause*). You are looking around you
(*pause*). What do you see? (*pause*). You can leave
(*pause*). Where do you go?'

This exercise can bring up symbolic issues about being confined, and having choices.

Fancy dress party

'You have received an invitation to a fancy dress party.

'Let an image come of your costume.'

It could happen that some thinking might intrude ('I could wear that Japanese dressing-gown'). Even then, some spontaneous aspects could be explored – colour, material used, size, position on page, missing features – which could yield relevant material from the subconscious.

MORE EXERCISES

The previous exercises in this book have been explained in some detail so the reader is able to become familiar with the basic structure and use the exercises as a 'hook' to the imagination, away from the 'thinking' mode. Below, I offer a list of exercises without the extra explanation.

Photo album

'You are turning out a desk (*pause*). You find a photo album (*pause*). You sit down to look at it, turning the pages…one photo catches your eye.'

Car boot sale

'You are driving along. You see a car boot sale in a field (*pause*). You drive to its car park and enter (*pause*). You are looking at the different stalls… something draws your attention (*pause*). You take a closer look.'

River bank

'You are sitting on a river bank...watching the water flow by (*pause*). You notice something floating by...'

A walk

'You are taking a walk...looking about you (*pause*). Now, suddenly, a fog comes down (*pause*). You see nothing (*pause*). How do you feel? (*longer pause*). Now the fog lifts (*pause*). What do you see?'

Computer

'You switch on your computer (*pause*). There is one message in your in-box (*pause*). You open it…it says: "Go to the attachment" (*pause*). You do (*pause*). A picture emerges…'

The lighthouse

'It is dusk. You are walking on a path to a lighthouse (*pause*). You draw closer to the lighthouse and look up at it (*pause*). You enter it and begin to climb the stairs – up and up… and arrive at the top (*pause*). Outside, it is dark now…you see the beam of light, as it rotates (*pause*). Now it shines on a particular place (*pause*). You look, you see what it illuminates…'

Art exhibition

'You are going to an art exhibition, walking through the main door (*pause*). You get your ticket…and you start looking at the paintings (*pause*). From one room to the next (*pause*). You come to a small room with just one painting on the wall…you go up to it…look at the label to its side…with the artist's name: it is your name (*pause*). You look closely at the painting…'

Pond

'You are standing near a pond…holding a fishing net (*pause*). You dip the net into the pond (*pause*). In a while, the net feels heavy (*pause*). You lift it out of the pond, put it on the ground (*pause*). What do you see?'

A walk on the beach

'You are walking along a beach…the tide is going out…you notice something the tide has left behind (*pause*). You take a look at it…'

A bird

'Let an image come of a bird...'

An animal

'Let an image come of an animal...'

A castle

'You are walking up to a castle...you go in (*pause*). You walk from room to room (*pause*). You enter a room (*pause*). You find a surprise.'

Winter walk

'You are taking a walk…it has been snowing (*pause*). You notice a spoor in the snow (*pause*). You follow it…'

Spring clean

'You are turning out a room…maybe a cupboard…a chest of drawers (*pause*). You find something unexpected…'

Childhood memory

'Let an image float up of a childhood memory…'

A relationship

'Let an image float up of a relationship…'

A seed

'There is a sale of unmarked seed packets at your garden centre (*pause*). You buy a packet…you plant the seeds (*pause*). What comes up?'

A house

'Let an image come of a house…'

A tunnel

'You see a tunnel ahead of you (*pause*). You enter the dark tunnel...you walk...ahead of you, a light (*pause*). You continue to the light (*pause*). You leave the tunnel (*pause*). What do you see? Feel?'

Toyshop

'You are out shopping. You pass a toyshop (*pause*). You go in, walk about, looking at the toys (*pause*). You may be drawn to one in particular.'

Image in the round

The group members sit in a circle. Each has a piece of paper in front of them. 'Without thinking, draw a shape on your page (allow 30 seconds to do this) and pass it on to your right.' Continue until the page returns to the first person, with additions from each group member. Debrief, starting with the producer of the first shape.

Much can occur about personal space, about the kind of shapes contributed, about feelings evoked.

Walk-sound

'You are taking a walk…you hear a sound behind you (*pause*). You turn round…'

Sounds can bring up spontaneous images. Similarly, a piece of music being played may evoke rich material. Any of your senses can be utilised.

Pioneer

'Allow an image to emerge of you, the pioneer...'

Separation, loss, change

'Sit comfortably...relax...take some easy regular breaths (*pause*). Clear your mind of thoughts (*longer pause*). And now, see what image emerges when I say "separation, loss, change"?'

This exercise is suitable for any ending – end of a course, bereavement, divorce, change of job, child leaving home, move to a new town/country/area – which needs acknowledging.

Write your own exercises, ideas and comments here:

CHAPTER 2

Art Therapy Exercises to Explore Individual Issues and Group Dynamics

The purpose of the following exercises is to explore the image individually and link it to the group dynamic, thus giving an opportunity to become aware of the groups dynamic, and change it as appropriate.

For example, with the circus image (see p.62) one member's image is the tightrope walker. In group dynamics, he is seen as the risk taker and the group colludes in letting him carry that role. Thus, they needn't take risks and he has to take them all. With awareness may come the notion that he may want to tap into other aspects of himself – he may want to be the clown or the ticket-seller.

The group members need to take back their projection of the tightrope walker – now some of them can take risks and the group becomes more aware, more balanced and healthier; it can function more effectively.

These activities follow a similar process to the activities designed for exploring individuals within a group, but operate on a group level.

Such exercises may be fruitfully applied with families, support groups (for bereavement, abuse, addiction, women), prisoners, student groups and so on.

EXERCISES

Circus

Before the session: prepare large sheet of paper big enough for all participants – maybe smaller pieces taped together. Put the large sheet down, surrounded by felt tip pens, chalks, crayons, etc. Participants have their eyes open.

'You are at the circus (*pause*). Where are you? (*pause*). Who are you?' (*longer pause*).

You may want to draw aspects of the circus and you in it (*pause*).

'You have x minutes (*pause*). You have one minute to finish.'

Individuals share their input, for example acrobat, clown, spectator. Then the group dynamic is explored.

Maybe one member manifests one aspect of his or her personality predominantly (e.g. the clown). Others may let him or her carry that role for the group, preventing them from tapping into that aspect in themselves. The projection needs to be taken back, consciously. Then everyone can be the 'clown' now and then.

A useful exercise with families, teams, groups, etc. – who is the rebel, the truant, the know-all? etc. preventing those aspects from surfacing in others. The image keeps, may be referred to again, and any change noticed. It can be less threatening to talk about – the clown – than the person.

A cake

You are baking a cake together.

'Close your eyes…let an image come up for you about a part you want to bring to the cake-making (*pause*). Now, gently open your eyes and portray this item.'

Members of the group share the image of their contribution on an individual level. Then the group dynamic element is explored.

The symbolism of, say, bringing the cake tin, the flour, the cherry on the icing, of bringing more than one item – what does that say about the person, and what she or he might carry for the group.

Swimming pool

Before the session, prepare a large piece of paper. On it, outline aspects of the swimming pool, such as the deep end, paddling pool, diving boards, changing rooms, café, deckchairs, entrance, lanes, etc.

> 'This is the swimming pool (*pause*). Put yourself wherever feels right for you (*pause*). You have five minutes (*pause for four minutes*). You have one minute to finish.'

Work with individuals, and the group dynamic. Interesting and relevant insights can evolve.

Similar themes for group, individuals and the group dynamic include:

- 'toytown'
- 'in the park'
- 'at the seaside'
- 'a picnic'
- 'a group island'.

A house

(two hours needed)

Before the session, collect different-sized and different-shaped boxes (supermarkets, shoe shops, stationers, etc. may be helpful). Collect collage material, coloured paper, tape, glue, scissors, etc. A longer session is required to make the house and work with the resulting image.

During the session, spread out the materials.

'You are making a house. You have one hour. Please try not to talk, to stay connected with your task.'

(*After approximately 50 minutes*) 'You have five minutes left.'

I don't offer a tea-break at half-time. It is a 'break' and disconnects the imaging process.

Work on each 'house'. Ask participants to place their 'house' as part of the village. Work on what ensues, what comes up for the group dynamic.

An enjoyable, creative exercise which can lead to multi-layered insights.

For staff groups, student groups, families, residential groups, etc.

No mortgage needed!

Once upon a time

Before the session, prepare a piece of paper long enough for four or five people to sit in front of it. (Lining paper does this well.)

Lay down the paper. Get the participants to sit down before it, then say:

> 'Draw a story which starts with "Once upon a time".
> A story about some being, some creature of your
> choice. Start your story on the part of the paper
> in front of you, and then see where else you might
> want to go with it.
>
> 'Once upon a time...'

If, after a time, no one continues drawing and joining images, repeat that they can take their story to other parts of the paper.

The purpose of this exercise is three-fold:

1. To give participants the opportunity to tap into their allegorical world of myth and fairy tale.

2. By using other people's images for their own symbolic projections, to look at personal issues of boundaries and risk-taking.

3. To explore your own fairy tale, and its links to yourself.

Mandala

Mandala is the Sanskrit word for 'circle'. It is a symbolic diagram depicting dualistic and complementary principles of the universe. Jung introduced the mandala to therapy as a dialogue between the conscious and unconscious. Mandalas are about balance, wholeness and integration. Based on visualization, a microcosm of the self in the here-and-now can emerge. Mandalas may be used in groups to disclose both the individual and group dynamic.

Allow long enough to paint and debrief the mandala. Two hours suits. Paints can be used. Participants make a large paper circle and put it on the floor; art material is placed around it. The participants decide to draw or paint freely anywhere on the circle. There will be half an hour for painting. No talking.

Debriefing on both individual and group levels, again, we can see how truths emerge when we are spontaneous. It can happen that members sit opposite those who carried opposite aspects of themselves – pairs of opposites (e.g. the introvert opposite the extravert). We marvel at the emerging intuitive wisdom of art therapy, and then, as we move on, we can say: 'But of course, how else could it be?' – integration of both forms of wisdom can occur.

Frequently, archetypal symbols emerge, containing individual meanings as well as some aspect of the collective unconscious. Sometimes mandalas – as indeed all images, contain the potential of expressing something from the past as well as something as yet unknown, to reach awareness later – the image knows before the event.

Mandalas can be used both by groups and individuals, as a symbolic illustration of some opposite aspects needing attention, integration, balance, resolution.

Write your own exercises, ideas and comments here:

CHAPTER 3

Further Inspiration for Art Therapy Exercises

Dreams

Art therapy exercises tend to tap into daydreams. Dreams, whilst we are asleep, are symbolic images from the unconscious. Thus they can give us significant material if brought up, produced in picture form and explored.

As dreams are, as yet, unknown to us a reverence, a respect, needs to be shown when working with them:

> I have spread my dreams under your feet. Tread
> softly because you tread on my dreams.
>
> *WB Yeats*

Working with a recent dream: a recurring dream, a significant dream, may be productive.

A colleague, Robin Shohet, would enquire what was going on for the client on the evening of the dream; what was the most dominant feature; what the least noticeable; what was drawn first, last, left out (*Dream Sharing*, Turnstone Press, 1985).

There are those who interpret dreams. Again, I prefer the person-centred approach. Even with archetypal themes, there are aspects that are unique to the client which need honouring. Cherries, for example, are traditionally associated with the mother's nipple, but they might have a different association for the client – let her or him speak!

Art exercises to work with a symptom

'Focus on a symptom you have now…or a symptom that reoccurs (*pause*). Where in your body is it (*pause*). How does it feel? (*pause*). How does it make you feel?

'Be aware of this symptom in all its details (*pause*). Now, let an image float up for you of your symptom.'

Two relevant questions may be:

1. What does your symptom help you avoid?
2. What do you gain out of having your symptom?

It is well documented that a high percentage of symptoms can be psychomatic. So, it may be productive to offer symptom image-work; it can lead to recovery.

There are doctors who use imaging with symptoms. Bernie Siegal MD, in his book *Love, Medicine – Miracles* (Rider & Co., 1999, ISBN 978-0712670-463), offers imaging around the diagnosis and treatment of the patient. If the image about the treatment is negative the treatment is stopped, and is continued if the perception of the treatment on a conscious level becomes, after exploration and dialogue, positive. Siegel advocates that all doctors should carry art material in their medical bag!

Often when I have a symptom, I let an image come of it. Often, with ensuing insight, the symptom retreats, and a visit to the doctor is unnecessary. Tell it to your local doctor!

EXERCISES

Working with images therapeutically may be used with large groups, small groups or individuals. Below are two examples of how to work in a group of two or three individuals. If you are clear about your purpose, the appropriate format will come to you.

The tree

Work in pairs, take a different colour marker each. Without talking, draw a tree together.

This activity provides an opportunity to think about who fetches the paper, who starts, who leads, who follows, who does roots, thorns, etc. – all good stuff. Finish drawing after about three to four minutes, when enough has been drawn. Then explore.

A conversation without words

Working in pairs – or threes or fours, each participant gets a different colour marker, and without talking has a conversation on one piece of paper (don't write words). Again, who gets the paper, its size, colour – was it negotiated? How were the markers chosen? Who begins, who goes over other people's marks, who stays in their corner?

I remember offering this exercise to a couple. It was the first session: one drew marks on one side of the paper, the partner made marks on the other end – a big, empty space in between. They came to improve their relationship. The picture became their contract, went up on the wall. The picture on their last session showed the two sets of marks touching, intertwining in a gentle dance.

One advantage of image-work is that it is private: up on the wall, no one else knew the meaning. Each week we could talk in terms of 'the red marks' and 'the green marks', easier than making eye contact with the counsellor. And I can visualize the image years on, although the exact words have vanished.

Calendar-based exercises

This is a scopeful resource for the facilitator for appropriate imaging exercises. Dates in the calendar lend themselves to art therapy exercises. It is best to offer them on or
near their actual date, in harmony with the energy of that
time. Be aware of your client-group when offering such
exercises. We live in a multi-faith, multi-cultural society
in which different clients might use different calendars.
Working with respect for the client enhances trust. For
example, New Year with your clients in mind. (Note that
the Hindu New Year, Chinese New Year, Jewish New Year,
Islamic New Year, and Roman Secular New Year all fall at
different times of the year.)

Some examples during the course of the year are listed
below.

- Imbolc – 2 February – a time of rest, *pause* and pu-
  rification. A time to dream your life. Light return-
  ing, a feeling of freedom. Creativity can emerge.

- Valentine's Day – 14 February.

- Spring equinox – 20–23 March – balance. Quick-
  ening of energy. The egg – symbol of life.

- April Fool's Day – 1 April. The fool/trickster.

- Mother's Day.

- Easter.

- Beltane – 30 April – beginning of summer.

- May queen – sexual licence – maypole.

- Summer solstice – 20–23 June; longest day.
  Time of transformation and renewal. Abundance,
  warmth, love.

- Lammas – 1 August; first fruits of harvest. Corn dolly.

- Autumn equinox – 20–23 September; harvest festival. Balance.

- Samhain – 31 October. Beginning of winter. Burning away dross. Veils between worlds are thin – honour the ancestors.

- Winter equinox – 20–23 December; maximum darkness. The sun is born from the womb of night. From now on, light increases, a turning point.

- Yule – 25 December.

An Easter egg hunt

'You are setting off on an Easter egg hunt…you
are in a wood…searching (*pause*). In a thicket
something glistens (*pause*). It is an egg…it cracks
open (*pause*). What do you see?'

Jewish Passover

The story of the Exodus – from slavery, to freedom, has
good imaging potential.

EXERCISES USING DIFFERENT MATERIALS

Sometimes, a facilitator, the client or both, might want a change from art work to another form of creative expression. Here are a few ideas for individual work in a group, or one-to-one.

Plasticine

Participants sit in a circle. Place coloured plasticine in the centre.

> 'Take a piece of plasticine. Without thinking, let your hands form the plasticine, shape it. You have two minutes.'

Each member talks about his or her creation. Often, there is amazement at the apt projections which emerge from something made so quickly. Even one minute is long enough!

The same exercise may be offered with long coloured pipe-cleaners from craft departments.

The following exercises may be offered in individual sessions.

An object

Ask participants (or clients) to go into a garden or park, walk about slowly and collect an object they are drawn to. Bring it to the next session.

Again, each member talks about her or his object, and may well identify a link.

I remember selecting a small, smooth stone. On one side it had a crack. A scar. I wept. My pain – the scar of the Holocaust, still part of me.

(Sometimes, when appropriate, as tutor, I would participate in an exercise. I was told that my trust and congruence were appreciated by the students.)

Buttons

Before the session, collect numerous buttons of diverse colours and sizes. You may find assorted bags of them at markets, car boot sales, etc.

You are working with one client. They may be talking of a relationship, of a family issue, a work problem. When it seems right, you produce your button-container and spill out a good number.

You invite the client to reproduce the scene – the family, the staff, group, whatever – with the buttons. You interject. Maybe: 'The mother-button is larger than your button.' 'Your sister is nearer to mother than you.' 'What colour is this button?' 'You are not there.' 'You have moved this button,' etc. A kind of button-psychodrama, which can produce significant insights.

Picture postcards

Before the session you collect a good number of diverse picture postcards, pictures from magazines, etc. You place them on the floor, face-up.

Invite the participant(s) to look at the cards – and pick up one to which they feel drawn. Then they, in turn, speak of their picture-card. They may well recognize the projection.

Here you provide ready-made images rather than evoking one with an art therapy exercise.

The materials needed for the above exercises, once collected, are easy to carry about with you. Part of your tool bag!

Collage

Collect a variety of materials to use in an exercise using collage. Here, working with the material the client has used can lead to insights (you may need silver foil for mother, black tissue paper for work, etc.).

If, by now, you have offered several of these exercises, not only your clients, but you too may have become more intuitive, creative, spontaneous and whole.

Write you own exercises, ideas and comments here:

CHAPTER 4

Working with Different Clients

Art therapy with children

Art therapy can be used effectively at every level of human development, provided that the practitioner works appropriately within the clients' environment and at their level of comprehension. To illustrate, I bring a small sample of working with children when I worked as a school counsellor in a comprehensive school in Brixton, and also adults with learning difficulties, which took place at an occupational training centre.

Peter

Peter is 14, referred for lateness and truanting. I suggest he draws a tree. Carefully and slowly he does the roots, then a little tree, then a big tree. I point to a bird, flying:

> 'That's a bird, flying. It is worried, it doesn't know where its nest is – in this tree or in the one nearby or the one at the top.'

After a long pause Peter says, 'I don't know where to live; I'm with my uncle and I want to go to my dad's, and maybe I'll have to stay with my sister.' Peter, normally uncommunicative, was able to talk about himself, prompted by the bird–tree analogy. He went on, 'If I knew where I was going, I could settle down. When I don't know, I worry, I can't sleep, I can't get up and get myself to school, and I hang about with other kids and get into trouble with them.' A vicious circle.

Peter returns the following week. I suggest he draw a room. He draws a room. 'My room,' he says. The window has bars. 'So that no one can come in.' The door has three locks. I point. 'So that no one can come in,' he says.

On the floor, a large figure. 'My friend.' I note a small nozzle on its shoulder and point to it. 'Oh, it's not a real person – it's one you can blow up. You can't trust real people.'

No comment... We didn't meet again – he disappeared, no one knows where.

Derek

Derek is in Year 3 at school. Bright but lethargic. His mother, a single parent, lethargic, doesn't care. He was referred for lateness and laziness.

I suggest a drawing. He draws a pot with a lid on, standing on a fire. I point to the pot, 'That's me. The lid is "can't be bothered Derek".'

'And in the pot?'

'All the bits I can do.'

'And the fire?'

'That's me, the bit that can be bothered. The bit I want to keep burning.'

We stick the picture on the wall – our 'contract' – what Derek needs to do to keep the fire burning. No ten school reports could have put it better!

The picture is a safe, accurate, private term of reference as I ask after the pot, the fire, the lid and the bits in the pot.

Trudy

Trudy is 14, referred for persistent truanting. She is very bright, lives with mum and step-dad and is the oldest of eight siblings. Mother keeps her at home to help her. Trudy wants to be a nurse but needs school to get the necessary qualifications.

During our first session she draws: she is on a mountain. She gets pulled to one side by mother and the kids, to the other by teachers and nurses. Above her head she writes 'Help!' She wants to walk down the mountain and go where she wants to go. A graphic picture of Trudy. Much to sort out.

The following week I suggest she draws 'home'. 'Me at home' she calls it.

I point. Trudy says: 'This is me holding the baby.'

'And who is this, on the settee?' (in the middle of the picture).

'Dad – well, step-dad.'

'And what is this in his hand?'

'That is his belt.'

'His belt?'

'He belts me with it.'

Linda

Linda is 12. Six months ago her mother committed suicide. She has not talked about her mother's death, grieved.

I suggest she draws a house.

She does a cross-section of her home.

As I point, she says: 'This is my brother in his room, playing the guitar.' 'This is my room, this is the bathroom. This is where my dad sits with his girlfriend, watching the telly. This is the hall, the front door.'

I say: 'There is no kitchen is there?'

'Oh,'

'How's that?'

'Well, mum's gone. She used to cook. We talked...' and the floodgates opened, the grieving began.

This is a good example showing how important it is to work with a missing aspect, often leading to a crucial breakthrough.

How to redress the balance with children like Peter, Derek, Trudy and Linda – and the rest. Often I feel frustrated, sad.

At least working with art is non-threatening, visible, quick, safe sharing, releasing strong feelings, and leading to more self-awareness, and the pleasure of the creative experience is a bonus. Amazingly, with so much stacked against them and not of their doing, some do succeed. They warrant OBEs.

Art therapy with adults with learning disabilities

Several years ago I worked at a training centre for adults with learning difficulties. Here are some examples to show what we did.

The training centre is for trainees over the age of 19, with a wide range of learning disabilities. I visited on one day per week to work with small groups in the art room.

Rose is 39 with Down syndrome. She lives in a hostel. On my first day I arrive and set out the art materials. Rose, Lucy and Di arrive. I suggest they draw whatever they want.

Rose says she wants to draw a church. She says, 'I can't draw, will you draw it for me?'

I say, 'Yes, you can!' 'Just draw your church however you want.'

Lucy draws a garden, Di draws flowers.

Rose has drawn a large church. 'You see, you can draw,' I say. She is smiling. She draws two figures. 'That's me and John. It's our wedding.' (It is the picture on the cover of this book.) Whilst colouring in, she talks about the hostel, how she feels, about life there.

The next week, Rose, Lucy and Di are waiting outside the door. I say, 'You've remembered.' 'Yes.' (Often they are seen as people who can't remember.)

Ken arrives. He draws his family and tells me all about them whilst he draws. Rose's brown felt-tip runs out of ink. I suggest paint. She experiments by mixing paints, she makes brown, looks pleased; earlier she had said she can't use paint. She has finished the church. She draws John and Rose and a card for John.

Ken draws a disco – his brothers and himself, talking about them, how he feels. The following week Rose wants to make a picture 'for the competition' – 'I'll draw flowers.' She decides to draw them first, then the 'real' picture. Lucy draws a garden each week – the allotment, the flowers, the trees.

Di draws a door. Then a man, 'That's the postman. He has a letter for me.' She draws a letterbox in the door, makes a slit with scissors. She makes an envelope and pushes it through the letterbox. 'The letter is from my mum. She's in Australia.' She tells me that she wants to hear from mum. She cries, then talks about missing mum.

The next week Rose is sulking, angry. 'John has gone off me.' She thinks for a while. 'I want to draw a pattern.' She gets red paint and a large sheet of paper. She makes large zigzag lines across the page. Then, with black paint, she makes large dots. She repeats the pattern until the page is full. She is calming down – almost as if her zigzag and black blobs have let her anger out on paper.

The next week Lucy draws her garden, with a little house to one side. I point to it. 'Mum was in the house. Now she's gone. I stay in the garden, away from the empty house.' She cries, talks about mum and how she feels without her.

Rose makes a collage of domestic objects cut out from magazines. 'These are for our home, John and me.' She does another collage of cut-out houses. 'Which one shall we live in?'

I ask the centre's manager if we can put up an exhibition of the trainee's art work at the end of term. She agrees. The students are pleased. Up go the pictures for all to see. The artists are like Cheshire cats!

To summarise:

- Ken, while repeatedly drawing pictures of his family was able to talk about them, and about his own feelings to be in that family. Previously he had been unable to communicate on a personal level. Also, he improved his drawing skills and grew to enjoy drawing. He interacted well with the other trainees, looking at their art work and commenting.

- Di discovered she could paint, and enjoyed it. She was able to cry about her mother's absence, which she had bottled up.

- Lucy, after several weeks of avoiding the loss of her mother by drawing the garden, being in the garden, was able to return to the house and express her feelings.

- Rose could talk of her hopes to be with John, to marry him and set up home with him, whilst also acknowledging her frustration at life in the hostel. She could express her anger by painting her pattern. She discovered she could draw, could use paint and enjoyed doing so. She could make decisions.

All the trainees discovered that they could make art, use their imagination. This gave them some confidence, a better self-image.

Whilst art-making, they could share personal thoughts and feelings, easier via the image than eye to eye. They did not need to be given a 'theme'; they were still connected to their child-like imaginations, to know what they needed to express pictorially.

It made me sad: we are, in the main, born creative. Children in nursery schools paint fearlessly and boldly. By secondary school, the focus is on academic achievement, with less time to be creative. By adulthood we need art therapy exercises to re-activate our imaginations.

I learnt much during my stay at the centre. Top of the list, appreciating the child-like innocence of the trainees, making them congruent, transparent and open. I could trust all that they said, (politicians could learn!), whilst I drove home to a culture where there is hypocrisy, dissembling and avoidance.

I reaffirmed my conviction that art therapy is effective at every level of development, providing your interventions match the reality of the client and are within the framework of reference relevant to them.

CHAPTER 5

Some Guided Fantasies Devised by Students

The guided fantasies that follow were created by students on the College of North-East London Person-Centred Art Therapy Skills Diploma Course.

Find a comfortable place to sit. Close your eyes. Be aware of the chair you are sitting on and how it feels to be supported by it.

Let your mind wander, notice any sounds, in the room or outside.

Let your thoughts pass like clouds.

Bring your awareness to any sensations in your body.

When you are ready you may begin the guided fantasy.

You are walking up a hill.

Look around you, what can you see?

Are you alone or is someone with you?

Do you see other people around you? If so, what are they doing?

What can you hear?

What can you smell?

You see a barrier or crossing, perhaps it is a wall, a fence, a gate or a bridge?

You walk over to it and look at it.

Can you see over it, or is there an opening, and can you see the other side?

Make a note of what is in your view and how you are feeling.

What happens next?

Take notice of what you do next and how you are feeling, taking in the scenery and what is happening around you, if anything.

It is now time for you to return to where you started.

You take one last look at your surroundings.

You make your way back, looking around you.

You go down the hill, noticing how you are feeling.

You are now back to where you started.

Before coming back to the room…

If you like, gently move your head from side to side,

Wiggle your fingers and toes.

You may want to stretch!

When you are ready…

Bring yourself back into the room.

And in your own time,

You may open your eyes.

Portray your experience, in whatever way you want.

Chinar Abdulaziz

Reflecting Back…

Gently close your eyes…

Bringing your attention inwards…

Feeling your breath, touch the tip of your nose…

breathe in, breathe out…

Noticing your heartbeat…

You are now standing in front of a full-length mirror…

In whatever way you feel comfortable, you are noticing your physical presence…

Reflecting back…

Your reflection…is it speaking to you?

Can you see its message?

What are you wearing?

What role are you in?

What is coming up for you?

How are you feeling?

What is coming up for you?

Have a look around…

Where are you?

Notice if you are on your own…

Is anyone else with you?

It's time to gently turn away from the mirror…

And bringing your attention…your breath…back to the room…

Breathe in…breathe out…

Feeling your body resting against the chair…

Feeling your feet grounded on the floor…

Open your eyes…and when ready – image.

Charlotte Allyson

Close your eyes and make sure you are sitting comfortably

Listen to your breathing, feel your body move as you inhale and exhale.

When you exhale, feel your tension leave your body

When you inhale, feel your body relax.

You are sitting in your living room, when you receive a call. The person on the other end of the phone seems very excited about something.

They tell you they have found something you had lost long ago.

They have left it outside your house in a box.

You go to the door and find the box on the floor.

You pick up the box and bring it in.

You place the box carefully on the table.

And slowly you open it.

When you are ready, take some paper and draw what you see.

Beverley Asforis

Relax… Close your eyes…

You are cooking a special meal.

Where are you?

Look around…

What ingredients are in front of you?

Notice the smell…colour…and texture of them…

Are you cooking this meal for someone?

If so, who?

What for?

Look around the room… Take your time to see everything.

Now the meal is ready and on the table.

What is the meal you have cooked?

Notice how it looks.

How do you feel while you eat?

You have finished the meal now.

You get up and clear away the dishes.

Walk out of the room.

Come back to the room you are in today.

And when you are ready, open your eyes and start the image you have experienced.

Jan Coppen

'Now, I want you to imagine yourself on a terrace looking down into a garden. There are steps leading down into the garden, and as you walk down the steps you relax more and more, so you take a step down and relax, another and you relax deeper still, with each step until you finally reach the garden feeling calm and relaxed.

'You look around the garden and notice what is growing there. Take a deep breath and notice any fragrances from the plants.

'You begin to walk down the garden… Notice how the ground feels under your feet, what is it that you are walking on?

'You feel the elements against your skin, take a moment to look up to the sky… What do you see?

'When you bring your awareness back to the garden, take a look at anything that catches your attention (long pause).

'When you are ready, start walking back to the steps…

'With each step up you become more aware of your surroundings. When you are ready, come back into this room, open your eyes and create an image of any part of your journey into or around the garden.'

Jane Darougar

Find a comfortable position
Relax, closing your eyes.

Visualize yourself in a special place
Somewhere you regard as safe
No one knows this place but you
In this place you can be you.

How do you feel?

There are no expectations and no judgements
Here you can just 'be'
What does that feel like?

Look around you
What can you see?
Is there a smell?
Are there any sounds?
How do you feel?

You are now preparing yourself to return into this
room
You can take one last look at your special place
Slowly you leave
Feel yourself come back into the room
Feel the floor beneath your feet
When you are ready open your eyes.

Paulette Gibson

I'd like to invite you to make yourself comfortable

To close your eyes

To take regular breaths in and out pushing all
thoughts aside.

Now imagine that you are a bird

What kind of a bird are you?

Where do you spend most of your time?

Where is your home?

How do you feel as a bird?

Slowly you begin to take flight;

How does it feel to fly?

What are your surroundings?

Where are you going?

What do you feel?

What do you see?

Soon it is time to end your flight.

Where do you land?

Take a few moments to remember your flight as a
bird, and when you are ready, come back into the
room and portray your experience as a bird in an
image.

Dawn Malcolm

Visualization

Make yourself comfortable

I would like to invite you to close your eyes

Free all thoughts from your mind

Clear your mind of earlier thoughts and emotions which you had before you got here.

I would like you to breathe as you normally would

Notice how you inhale, notice how you exhale.

Become aware of your body, notice how your body is feeling

If there is tension in any part of your body, let it go.

Now, imagine you are walking down a path in a beautiful, natural environment. It may be familiar or unfamiliar, what is the weather like?

What can you see? Smell? Hear? Use all of your senses.

As you walk along the path it leads onto a beach, where are you?

What can you feel under your feet? You walk towards the edge of the water and pause as you notice the tide come in and out.

As you watch the tide come in, it brings something for you.

Something you may need, a gift, a desire, an unexpressed need perhaps, what is it?

You now watch the tide go out, this time it takes something from you, it may be something you no longer need, you don't want, may have never shared with anyone before, may be something that has been troubling you recently or for some time, what is it?

As you pause with your gift, and something, now taken away, how do you feel? Notice what's around you? Are you alone?

How does the air feel and smell?

Now it's time to go and you head back to the path, where you began.

As you return to the room, become aware of your body in the room, feel the room around you.

When you're ready, open your eyes and convey in any way, shape or form your journey or experience.

Charmaine Pollard

'Please close your eyes and take a deep breath in. Hold for a count of two and then, as you let the breath out, slowly and gently visualize all the thoughts and worries flowing out of you.

'You find yourself standing in front of a door, you notice the size, what it is made of and what colour it is. Is there anything on the door?

'You reach out and touch the door, and effortlessly it glides open. As you walk through the opening, you step into a room or space.

'What do you see?

'Is there anyone else there with you? Are they saying anything to you?

'You look in front of you and notice where you are. You look in front of you and notice some shelves. You walk over to them. There are lots of objects on the shelves but one object captures your gaze.

'It has a label on it saying your name and "for you".

'You are able to pick the object up and look at it.

'What is it made of, what does it look like, does it have colours, does it have a smell?

'How does it make you feel?

'As you are touching your object you know you have a choice.

'You make your choice.

'You turn and make your journey back to the door, you go through the door opening. As you do so, the door gently closes behind you.

'You are now back to (*fill in appropriate place*) where you can open your eyes.'

Stella Smith

A Final Word

I believe that to work most effectively with art therapy, both the facilitator and the client need to be connected to their creative, spontaneous aspects.

With no time to think, flying by your coat tails, the maximum potential of insight and awareness may be reached.

By being clear of your purpose, you are likely to offer the right structure at the right moment.

I hope, having read this book, and applied some of its ideas to yourself and others, the gate between your intellect and intuition may be well-oiled, leading to a more integrated way of being.

The blank pages following and elsewhere in this book offer space for you to include your own ideas, comments and experiences – this adds a reader-centred, person-centred element, which I prize.

I hope you have sufficient material and ideas to adapt and enrich your toolbag.

Bon voyage on your magical mystery tour of art therapy.

Write your own exercises, ideas and comments here: